The Chilling Voice

The Chilling Voice

by Michael Dugan
Illustrated by Rae Dale

THOMSON

NELSON

Chill Out is published by Nelson Thomson Learning and is distributed as follows:

AUSTRALIA
Nelson Thomson Learning
102 Dodds Street
Southbank 3006
Victoria

NEW ZEALAND
Nelson Price Milburn
1 Te Puni Street
Petone
Wellington

First published in 2002
10 9 8 7 6 5 4 3 2 1
05 04 03 02

Text © Michael Dugan 2002
Illustrations © Nelson Thomson Learning 2002

The Chilling Voice
ISBN 0 17 010 530 X

Project commissioned and managed by Lorraine Bambrough-Kelly,
The Writer's Style
Designed by Leigh Ashforth @ watershed art & design
Series design by James Lowe
Illustrations by Rae Dale
Printed in China by Midas Printing (Asia) Ltd

Acknowledgements
Thank you to the teachers and students of St John's Primary School, Heidelberg; St Francis Xavier Primary School, Montmorency; Luther College, Wonga Park; and the Atchison and Burns families. Thanks also to Lynn Howie and the Stage 3 boys at Alstonville Primary School for their assistance in developing this series.

Nelson Australia Pty Limited ACN 058 280 149 (incorporated in Victoria) trading as Nelson Thomson Learning.

Contents

Chapter 1	A Very Scary Message	7
Chapter 2	Real Fear	15
Chapter 3	The Puzzle Unravels	21
Chapter 4	A Visit to the Police	29
Chapter 5	Just One of Those Things	37

Chapter 1

A Very Scary Message

'I'm going out to do some shopping,' Jim's mum said to him. 'Do you want to come?'

'Nah,' Jim replied. 'Shopping's pretty boring. I'd rather go over to Troy's house and play computer games.'

'Well, make sure you're back by lunchtime.
Your grandparents are coming,' his mum warned.

She picked up her car keys. And went out the front door, closing it behind her.

Jim put away the breakfast cereal and milk.

'I might as well ring Troy first,' Jim thought.
'He might not be at home.'

9

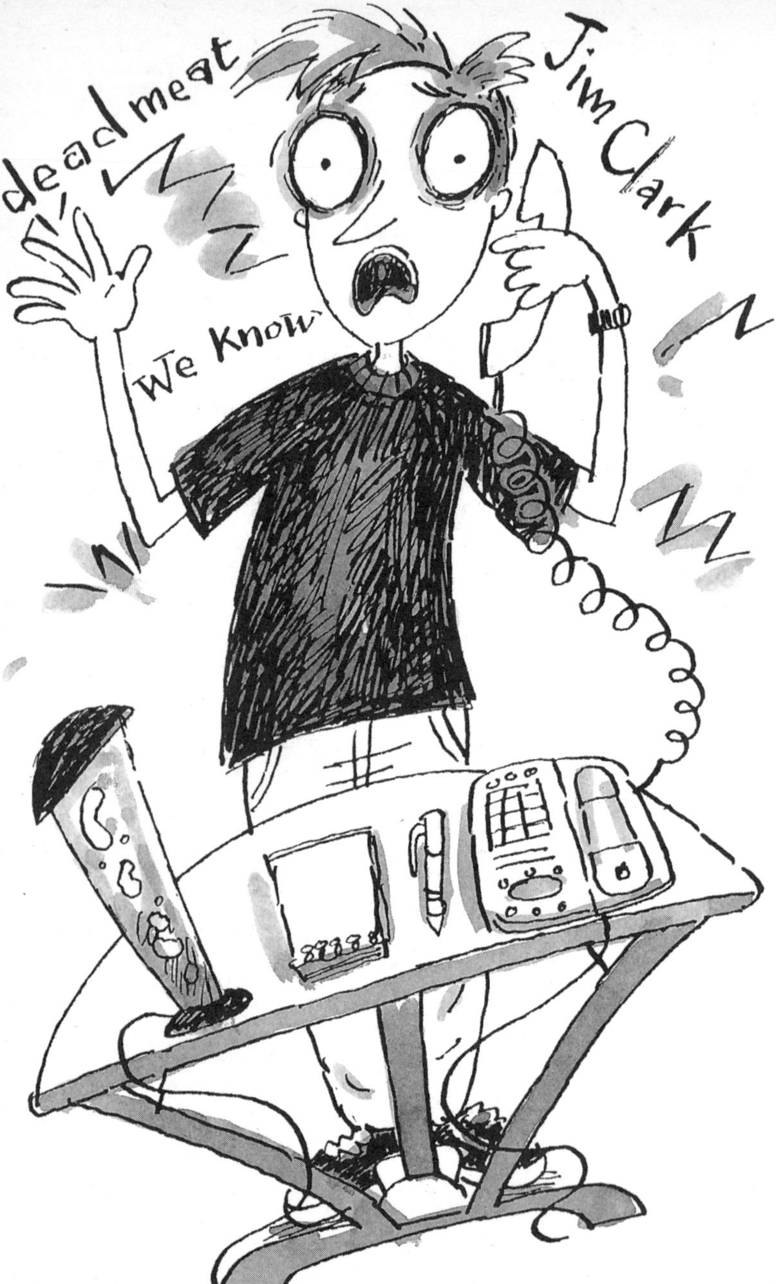
dead meat
Jim Clark
We Know

He knew Troy's number by heart. He dialled it.
But the ringing on the other end didn't sound right.

After a few rings, the phone was answered. But a
stranger spoke. And with a really menacing tone.

'If that's you, Jim Clark, then you're dead meat,'
the strange male voice said. 'We know what you've
done. And we're coming after you. You might as well
say goodbye to your friends. If you've still got any
left, that is.'

Jim stared at the phone. He was stunned. What was all this about? Could he really have heard what he thought he had heard?

And who was it on the other end of the phone? It certainly didn't sound like Troy's father. In fact he was sure that he'd never heard that chilling voice before. But it was *his* name that had been said in such threatening tones.

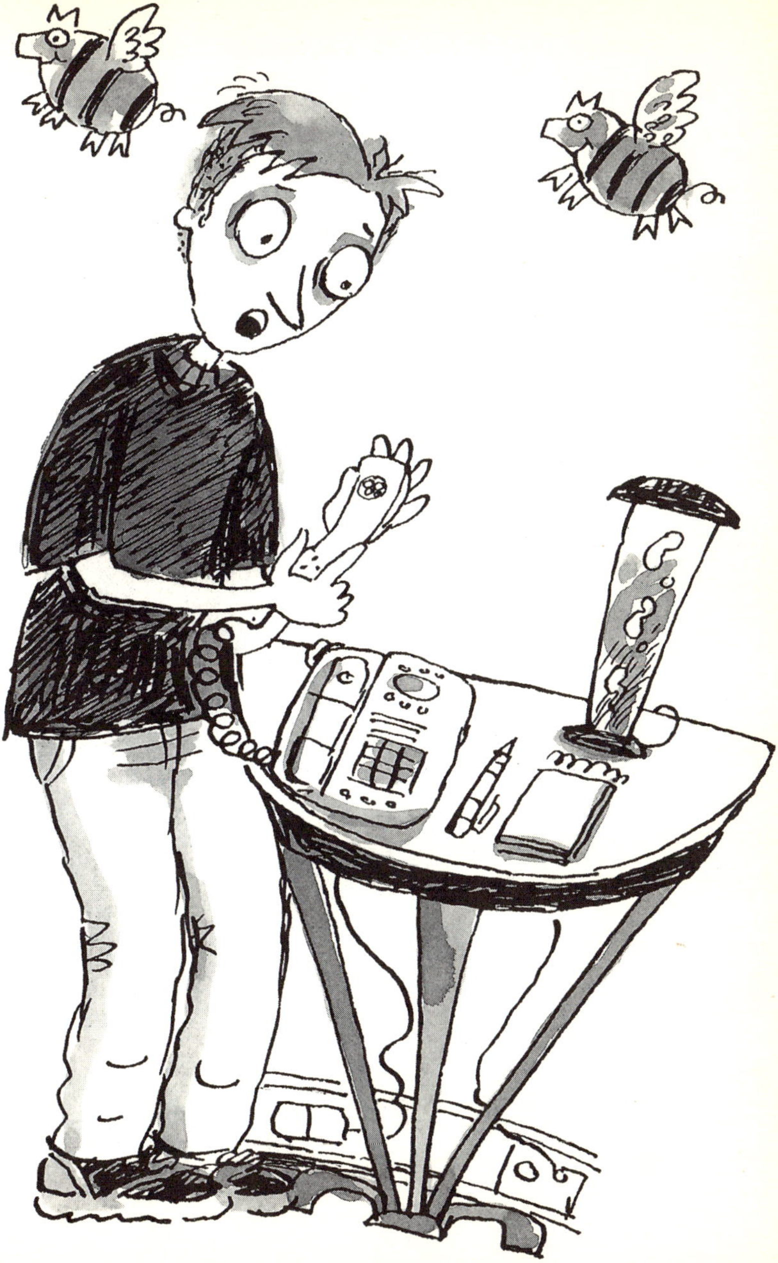

With shaky fingers, he rang the number again.
He checked each digit to make sure he had it right.
The same scary message was repeated, word for word.

There was a notepad by the phone. Jim grabbed a pen and wrote down the message, just as he had heard it.

Chapter 2

Real Fear

A branch blowing in the wind scraped against the window. Jim jumped! He felt his heart racing.

Hearing that nasty message had really rattled him. Was the owner of that voice already out in the garden, ready to get him?

There was no way he was going to stay in the house on his own. Whoever was out to get him might know where he lived. And come after him.

They might even have been watching the house and might have known that his mum had gone out.

They might already know that he was in the house on his own.

He went into the front room. And hid behind the curtain. He peered out of the window. He couldn't see anyone hiding in the garden.

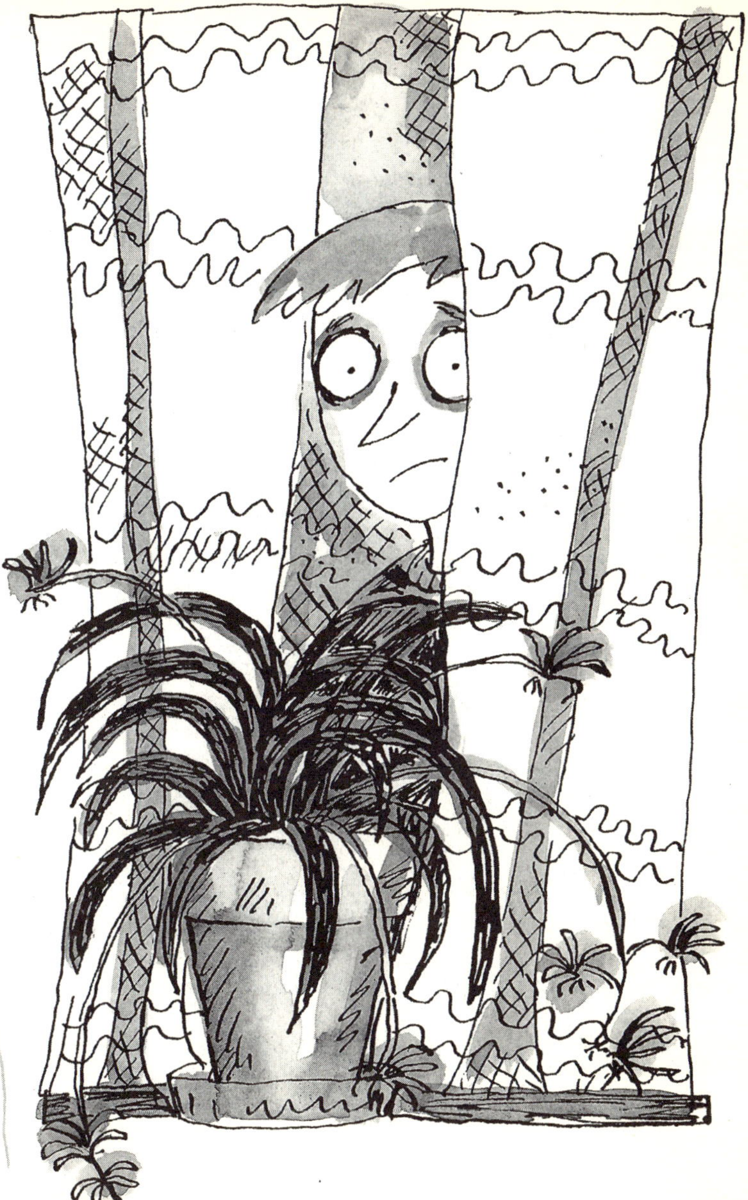

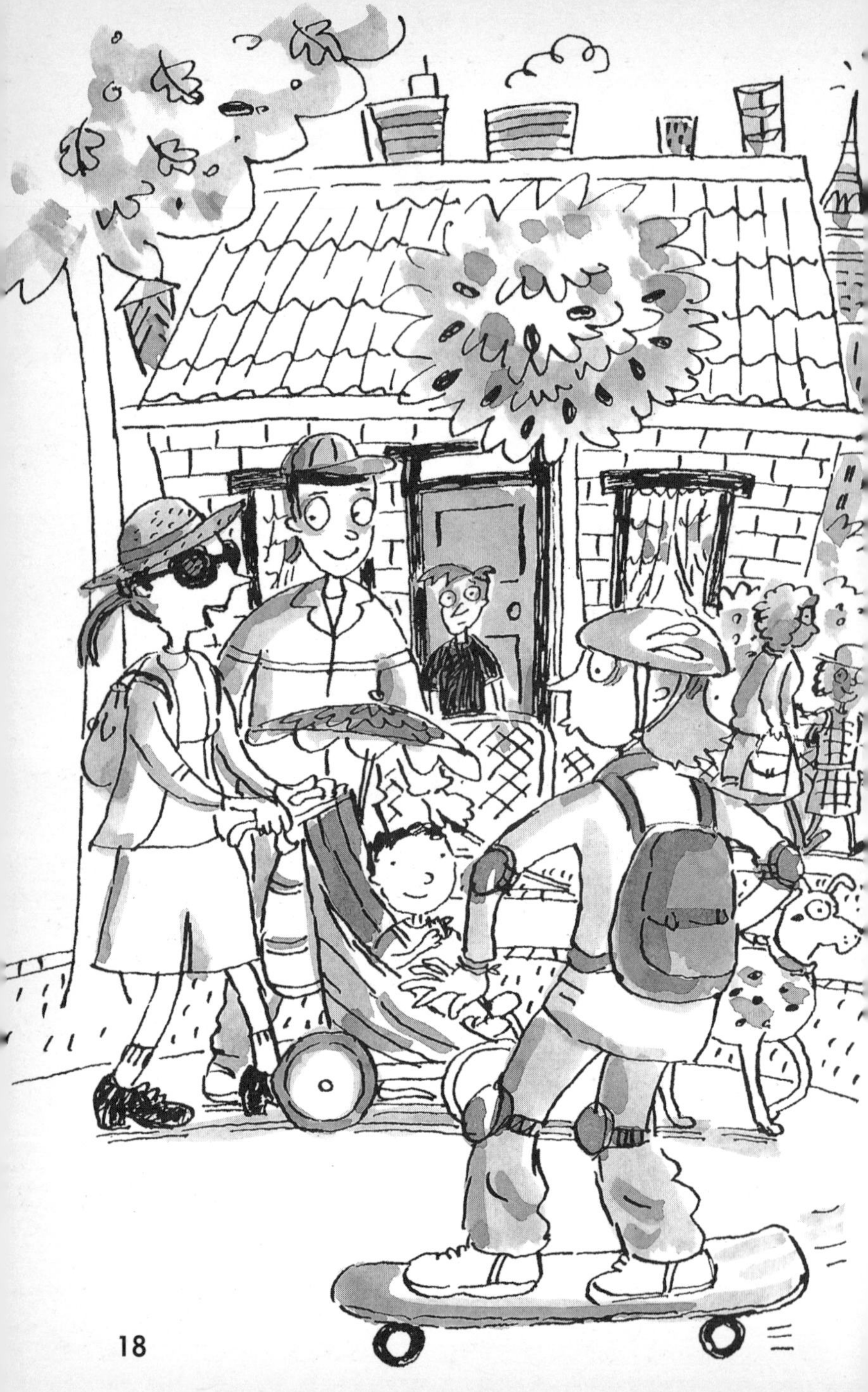

He opened the front door and slipped out. He closed the door behind him very quietly. Once outside he felt a sudden rising panic. He fought to control it.

Forcing himself to move, he walked to the front gate and looked out onto the street. There were lots of people out and about. He felt a bit safer.

But then he remembered a film he had once seen.
In it, a gangster had wiped out his enemy by turning
his car onto the footpath and running over him.
The gangster's car had sped off before anyone had
realised what had happened.

Jim turned from his own busy street, into a quiet side
street. He walked about fifty metres. Then he hid
behind a tree to see if anyone was coming after him.

No car turned into the street. And he felt safer again.

This street led to the street where Troy lived. But he'd
better not go to Troy's place now. He turned in the
opposite direction.

Chapter 3

The Puzzle Unravels

'Jim!' a voice called. Jim jumped. And his heart missed a beat. Then he saw Troy coming towards him on his scooter.

'I was just coming around to your place,' Troy said as he drew up beside Jim. 'Mum and Dad have gone to some boring old house auction.'

'Something weird's happened,' Jim said quickly. 'I've been getting a strange message on your answering machine.'

'You can't have,' Troy told him. 'We haven't had an answering machine for weeks. Dad reckons with four kids there's almost always someone home to answer the phone.'

23

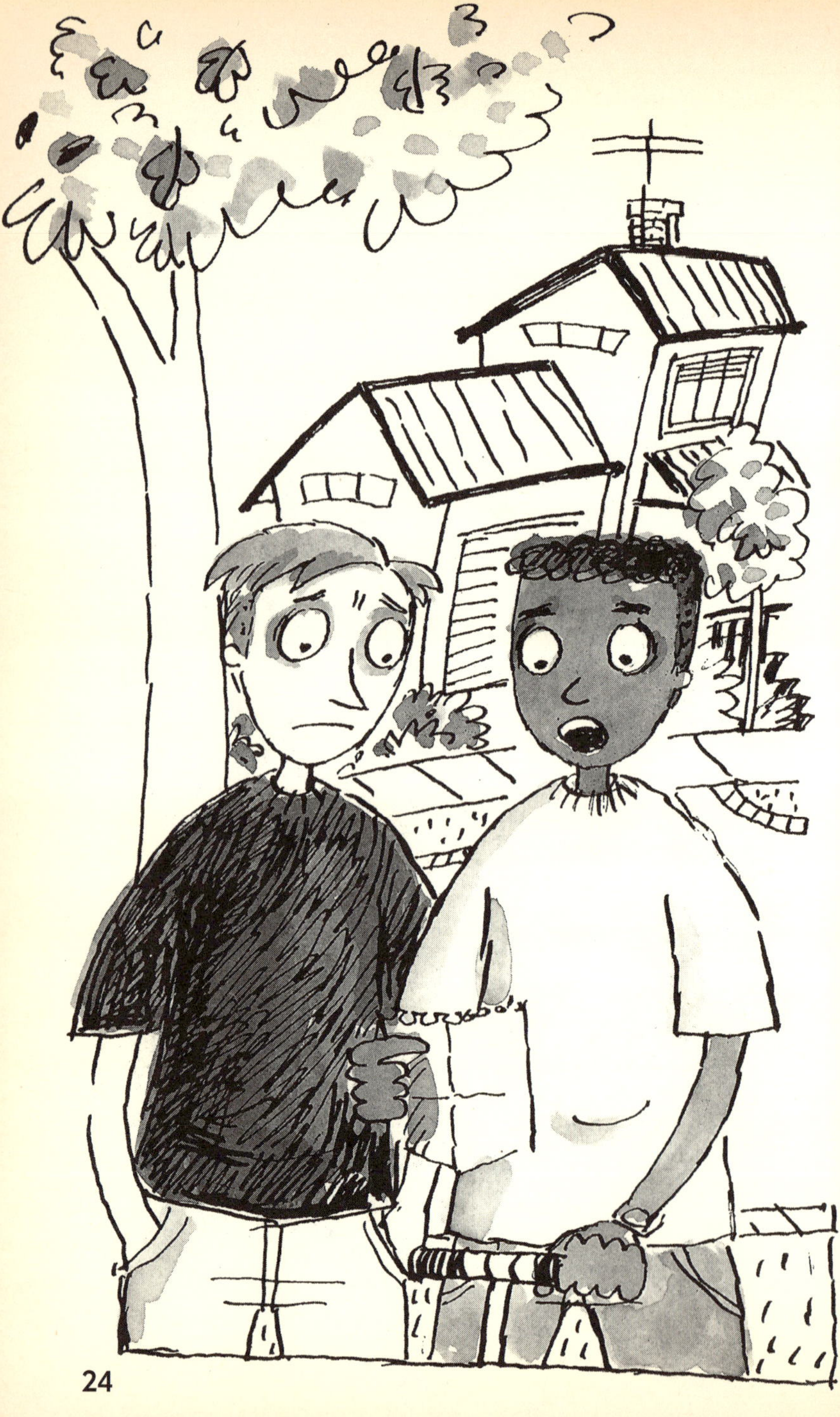

'But I just phoned your number. And there was a machine message. It was a mean-sounding guy threatening to kill me. I wrote down what he said.'

Jim pulled out the piece of paper he'd scribbled the message on. Troy read it quickly.

'That's impossible,' he said.

'But that's exactly what I heard,' Jim said. 'I even rang your number a second time. And got the same message.'

Troy suddenly grinned. 'I think I know what's happened,' he said. 'You must have rung our old number. We changed phone companies last week and got a new number. I thought my mum had told your mum the new number. But I guess she didn't.'

Jim grinned. At least he now knew that his best friend's dad wasn't trying to kill him.

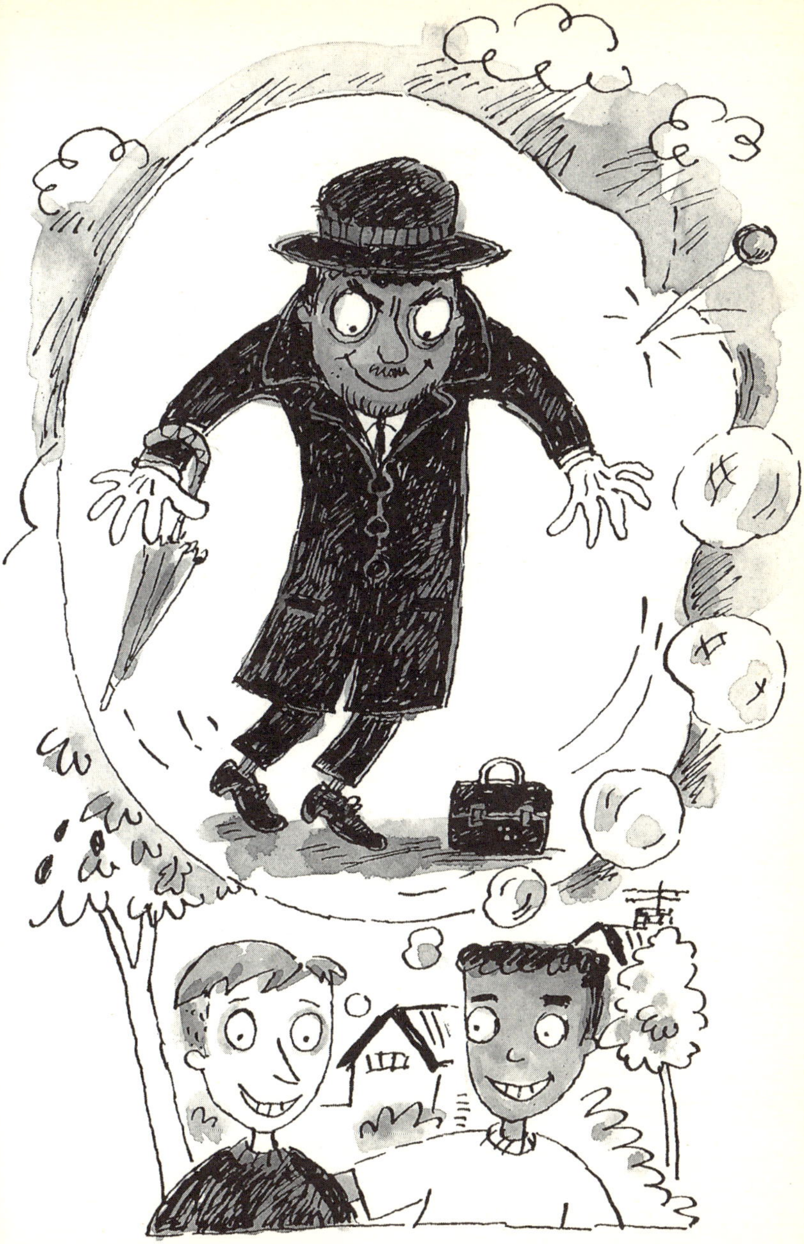

Jim thought hard. 'What we need to do is to find out who has your old number. Then we'll know who's threatening to kill me.'

'We'll have to go to the police,' Troy said firmly. 'This guy sounds like bad news.'

Chapter 4

A Visit to the Police

Troy walked his scooter with Jim beside him. They headed towards the police station.

Jim felt safer now that Troy was beside him. Surely whoever wanted to kill him wouldn't want a second victim.

Jim had never been in a police station before. A young policewoman asked him what he wanted.

Jim poured out his story. But the policewoman didn't believe him. So he showed her the note he had made of the message that was on the answering machine.

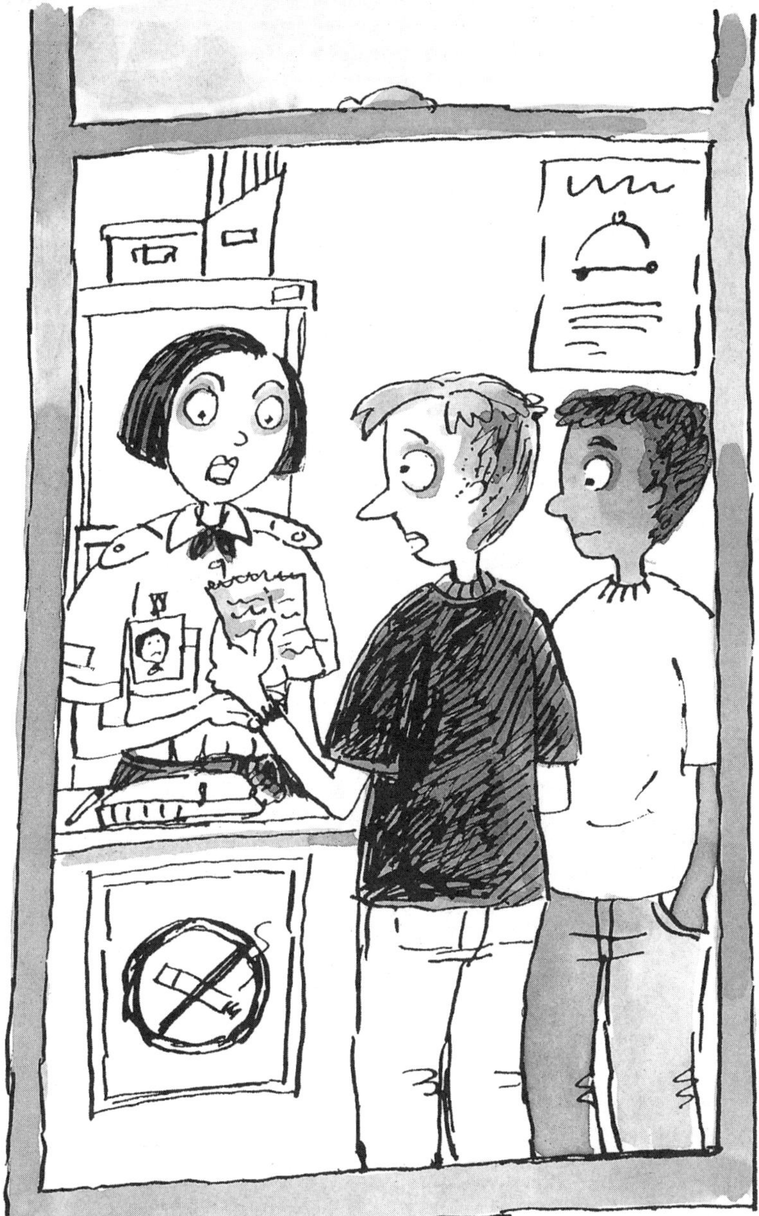

32

'Couldn't you try the number?' Troy asked. 'I can write it down for you.'

The policewoman offered him a pencil and paper. 'I don't mind doing that. But I think you're having me on. Or someone's having you on.'

She pressed the numbers and listened. Her face changed from one of disbelief to one of surprise. 'Well, the message is certainly there,' she said. 'Are you two sure you're not joking?'

'Of course we're not,' Jim replied. 'I only ran into Troy half an hour ago and, anyway, it's an adult's voice on the answering machine. And we're not adults.'

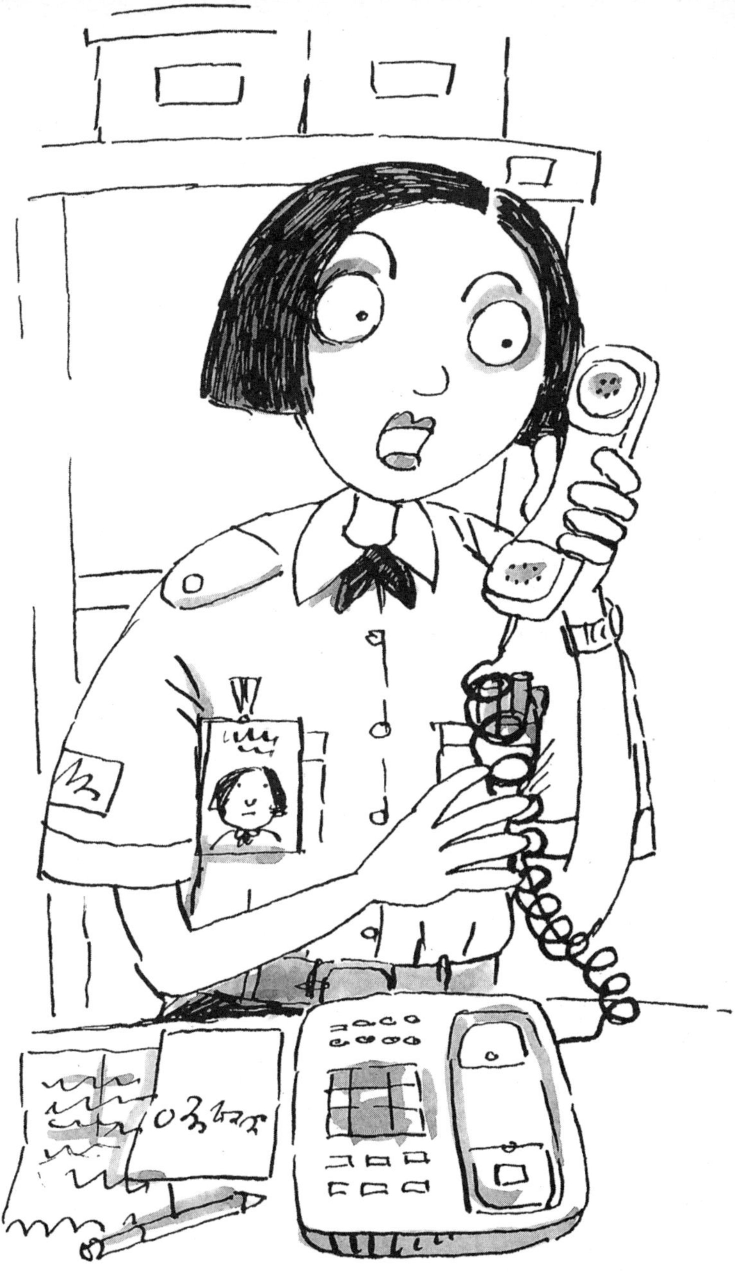

'All right, I believe you,' the policewoman said. 'We'll try to follow up on it. You two wait here.'

She left the reception area and went through a door.

Chapter 5

Just One of Those Things

Jim and Troy sat on some chairs in the reception area and waited.

Sometimes they whispered new ideas about the mystery to each other.

They had waited for about twenty minutes, when they heard lots of laughter coming from the other room. The policewoman returned to the reception area with a sergeant. He had a broad grin on his face.

'We've talked to the telephone company,' the policewoman said, 'and we're a bit wiser now. Troy's old number is now owned by an amateur theatre company.'

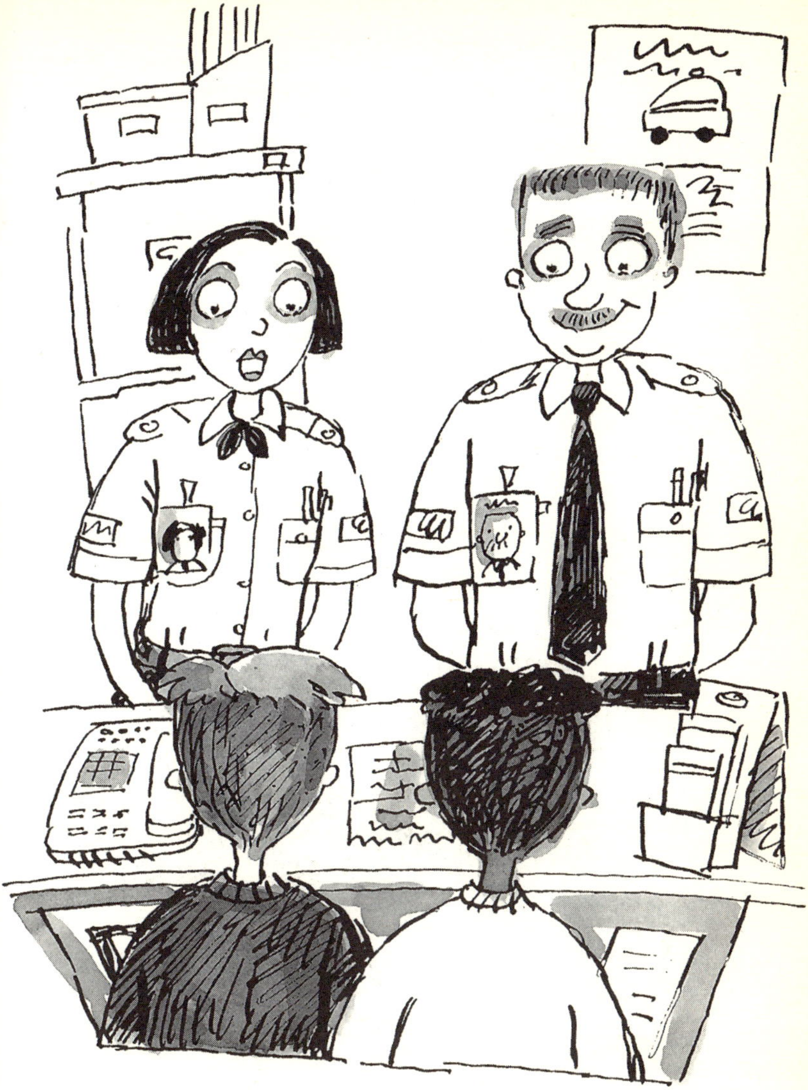

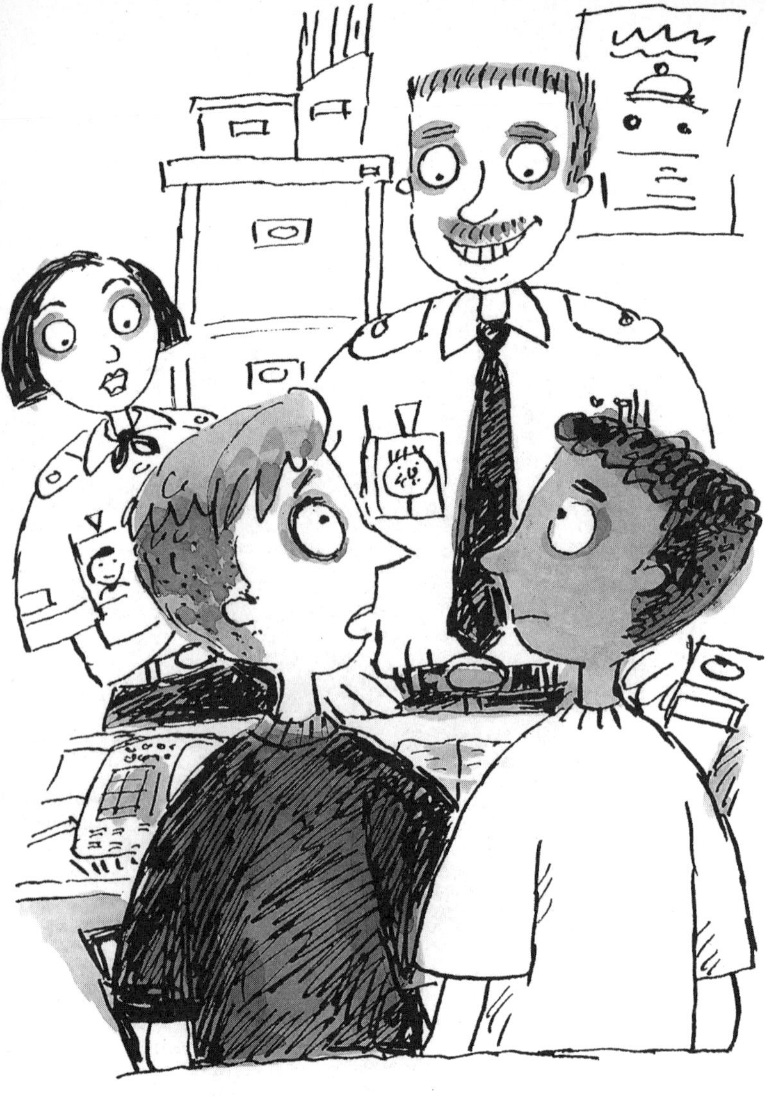

'So what?' Jim asked.

The sergeant's grin widened. 'Everything,' he replied. 'We contacted the theatre company. They told us they put the answering machine message on the new phone line because nobody knew the number. The message is going to be used for this scene in the play tonight. A drug smuggler has ratted on his mates, phones the number and hears the message.'

'And the criminal who dobbed in his gang in the play is called Jim Clark,' added the policewoman.

'Then it had nothing to do with me at all,' Jim said, feeling rather light-headed.

'Nothing at all,' the policewoman replied cheerfully. 'It's just one of those things that can happen when you have a fairly common name.'

Jim grinned at Troy in sheer relief. The boys thanked the policewoman, then they zipped off home feeling much happier indeed.

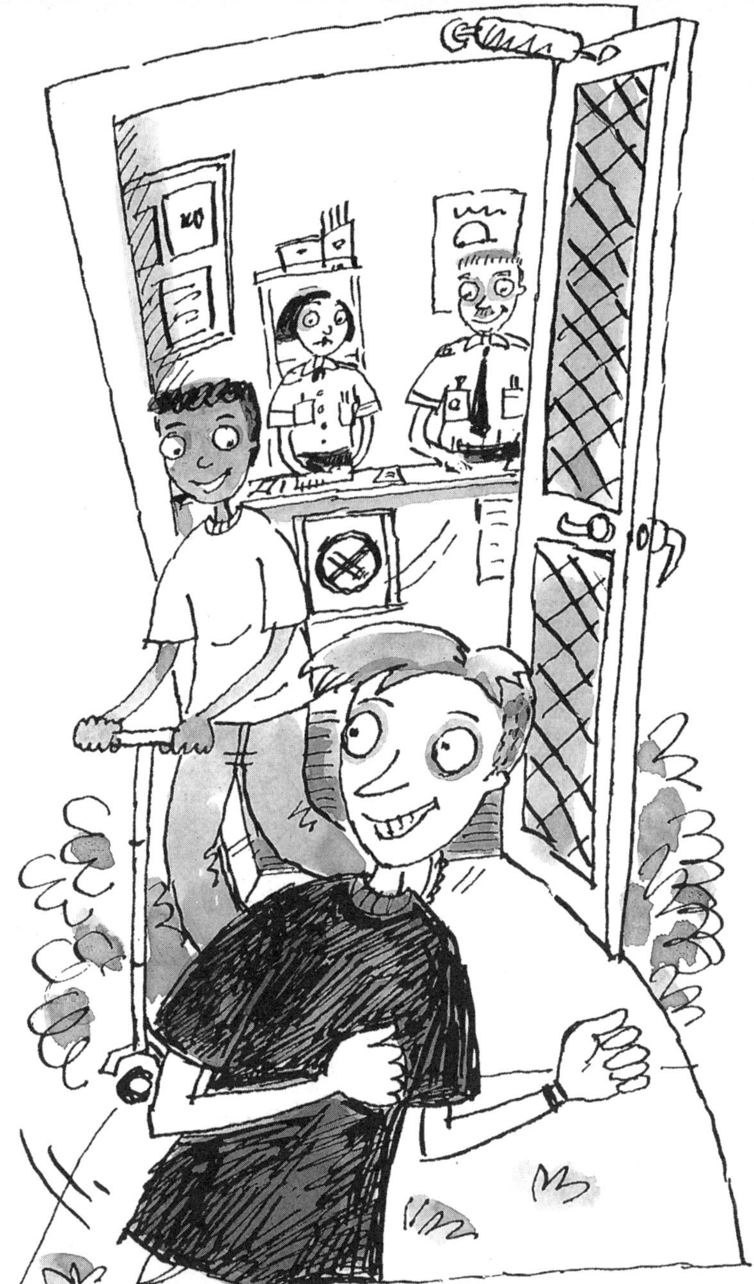

Michael Dugan

Author Snapshot
Michael **Dugan**

As a teenager, Michael Dugan once spent a night on his own in a remote house in the country. Turning on his radio, he heard on the news that a pair of murderers, who had escaped from prison, were believed to be hiding out in the same area.

Michael got very little sleep that night!

Rae Dale

Illustrator Snapshot
Rae **Dale**

Rae Dale lives in a country-like setting in the outer suburbs of Melbourne, Australia. She relies on her phone/fax/answering machine for keeping in touch with friends and taking messages for work.

But sometimes Rae receives calls from people who think she's Sharon, Brett or Sally – ooops – what a mistake!

When not returning phone calls, Rae illustrates children's books, potters in her garden, and tries to think up the perfect message to put on her answering machine to stop bossy callers.

Chill Out

Read **These**

Urgent Delivery by Dianne Bates

Revenge at Lake Happy by Jim Schembri

Private Keep Out by Christopher Stitt

A Prize Idiot by Bill Condon

In the Can by Christopher Stitt

The Reef Riders by Corinne Fenton

Fangs by Dianne Bates

Pitch Black by Janeen Brian

Tag Dag by Christopher Stitt

Warp World by Heather Hammonds

The Soccer Expo by Sue Cason

Zit Face by Chris Bell

Goose Head by Wendy Graham

One Battered Flathead by Peter Matheson

Big Day Out by Trish Lawrence

Getting Down and Dirty by Trish Lawrence

Real Guts by Jenny Pausacker

Tank by Jenny Pausacker

Crash Landing by Dianne Bates